ABORTION AND THE NEW LAW IN AMERICA:Abortion after Roe

TABLE OF CONTENTS

CHAPTER 1

Terminology

Abortion definitions

The abortion controversy is most frequently associated with the "induced abortion" of an embryo or fetus at some time during a pregnancy, which is also how the term is used legally.

Some also use the word "elective abortion," which refers to a claim to a woman's unfettered right to an abortion, whether or not she chooses to have one. The term elective abortion or voluntary abortion refers to the termination of a pregnancy before viability at the woman's desire, rather than for medical grounds. Miscarriage or abortion until the fetus is viable are both medical terms for abortion. After viability, physicians refer to abortion as a "pregnancy termination."

CHAPTER 2

History

Anti-abortion legislation is on the rise.
On request: AK, HI, NY, WA; threat to woman's health, rape or incest, or probable harmed fetus: AR, CA, CO, DE, FL, GA, KS, MD, NC, NM, OR, SC, VA; rape: MS; illegal: AZ, CT, IA, ID, IL, IN, KY, LA, ME, MI, MN, MO, MT, ND, NE, NH,
Abortion legislation in the United States before Roe
Unlawful (30)

In the event of a rape, it is legal (1)
Legal in cases where a woman's health is jeopardised
Legal in cases of woman's health hazard, rape or incest, or a potentially injured fetus
On-demand legal counsel
Abortion has been legal in the United States since European colonization. Methods for performing abortions early in pregnancy were described in the early 1800s. Abortion after quickening (the commencement of fetal movements, commonly felt 15-20 weeks after conception) was illegal under common law, but without codified legislation, the regulations were 'hazy.' Most states continued to use English common law on abortion after the United States gained independence.

Lord Ellenborough's Act of 1803 made abortion illegal by legislation in the United Kingdom, punishing post-quickening abortions with death and pre-quickening abortions with 'removal.'

Connecticut was the first U.S. state to criminalize medical abortion after quickening in 1821, and ten of the 26 states followed suit within 20 years.

In 1829, New York declared post-quickening abortions a crime and pre-quickening abortions a misdemeanor.

Some early regulations penalised not just the doctor or abortionist, but also the lady who hired them, according to some legal historians. Roe v. Wade decision

Roe v. Wade is the main article.

The composition of the United States Supreme Court in 1973

Prior to Roe v. Wade, 30 states outright forbade abortion, 16 states outright barred abortion except in certain rare circumstances (e.g., rape, incest, or a hazard to the mother's health), andstates permitted citizens to access abortions, and New York authorized abortions in general.

On January 22, 1973, the Supreme Court in Roe v. Wade overturned all of these bans and established criteria for abortion access. Roe recognized that a woman's right to privacy in obtaining an abortion "must be balanced against vital governmental interests in regulation." Roe defined the end of the first "trimester" (i.e., 12 weeks) as the threshold for state interest, such that states were forbidden from prohibiting abortion in the first trimester but permitted to impose increasing limits or complete prohibitions later in pregnancy.

The Supreme Court declared in Roe v. Wade that a Texas legislation prohibiting abortion except when required to preserve the mother's life was unconstitutional. The Court reached its ruling by holding that abortion and abortion rights are covered by the right to privacy (in the sense of the right of a person not to be encroached on by the state). In its decision, the court cited many historic judgments in which it had already identified a constitutionally implied right to privacy. The Court did not affirm a right to abortion in every case: state restrictions protecting fetal life after viability had both logical and

biological reasons. If the state is concerned about safeguarding embryonic life after viability, it may go so far as to prohibit abortion at that time, unless it is absolutely essential to save the mother's life or health. The Court ruled that there was a right to privacy, which includes the freedom to have an abortion. The court concluded that a mother has the right to an abortion until viability, which is determined by the abortion doctor. After viability, a woman can get an abortion for medical grounds, which the Court broadly construed to encompass psychological well-being.
A major question in the Roe v. Wade case (and in the broader abortion debate in general) is whether human existence or personhood starts at conception, birth, or somewhere in between. The Court rejected the attempt to decide this matter, noting: "We do not need to answer the complex question of when life starts. When those skilled in the fields of medicine, philosophy, and religion are unable to reach an agreement, the court is unable to speculate on the solution at this moment in man's evolution of knowledge." Instead, it opted to emphasise that historically, under English and American common law and laws, "the unborn have never been recognized... as people in the full sense," and so the foetuses are not legally entitled to the protections offered by the Fourteenth Amendment's right to life. Rather than claiming that human life begins at any particular time, the court simply stated that the state had a "compelling interest" in safeguarding "potential life" at the point of viability.
Bolton v. Doe

Doe v. Bolton is the main article.

According to Roe v. Wade, state governments may not restrict late abortions when "necessary to protect the life or health of the woman," even if it results in the death of a viable fetus.

The 1973 legal case Doe v. Bolton reinforced this norm, stating that "the medical judgement may be exercised in light of all factors—physical, emotional, psychological, family, and the woman's age relevant to the patient's well-being."   Women in the United States can lawfully choose abortion beyond viability when tests find abnormalities that do not cause a baby to die shortly after birth because of this provision for the mother's mental health.

Subsequent judicial rulings

The Court abandoned Roe's rigid trimester structure in Planned Parenthood v. Casey in 1992 but retained its key decision that women had the right to choose abortion before viability.

Roe ruled that abortion laws must be subjected to "strict scrutiny," the usual Supreme Court norm for impositions on basic constitutional rights. Casey instead used the lower, undue burden standard to evaluate state abortion restrictions, but emphasized the right to abortion as grounded in the general sense of liberty and privacy guaranteed by the constitution: "The Due Process Clause of the Fourteenth Amendment provides constitutional protections for a woman's decision to terminate her pregnancy. It states that no state may "deprive any individual of his or her

life, liberty, or property without due process of law."
The key term in the instances before us is 'liberty.'"
The Supreme Court continues to rule on this issue. It
made a judgment in the matter of Gonzales v. Carhart
on April 18, 2007, addressing a federal statute known
as the Partial-Birth Abortion Ban Act of 2003, which
President George W. Bush had signed into law. The
law prohibited intact dilation and extraction, which
opponents of abortion rights referred to as "partial-
birth abortion," and provided that anybody who broke
the rule may face up to 2.5 years in prison. By a close
5-4 vote, the United States Supreme Court maintained
the 2003 ban, marking the first time the Court has
authorized a ban on any sort of abortion since 1973.
Justice Anthony Kennedy wrote the judgement, which
was joined by Justices Antonin Scalia, Clarence
Thomas, and the two most recent appointments,
Samuel Alito and Chief Justice John Roberts.
In Whole Woman's Health v. Hellerstedt, the Supreme
Court ruled 5-3 on June 27, 2016, to overturn state
limits on how abortion clinics operate. The Texas
legislature approved abortion restrictions in 2013,
arguing that they imposed an unreasonable barrier on
women seeking abortions by forcing abortion
physicians to have difficult-to-obtain "admitting
privileges" at a nearby hospital and clinics to have
costly hospital-grade facilities. The Court agreed with
this approach and struck down these two provisions
"facially" from the legislation at issue—that is, the
provisions' language was unlawful regardless of how
they were interpreted in any practical circumstance.

The duty of determining whether legislation places an unconstitutional burden on a woman's right to abortion, according to the Supreme Court, falls to the courts, not legislators.

On June 29, 2020, the Supreme Court held 5-4 in June Medical Services, LLC v. Russo that a Louisiana state legislation, fashioned after the Texas provision at the heart of Whole Woman's Health, was unconstitutional. The Louisiana bill, like the Texas law, demanded specific conditions for abortion clinics that, if implemented, would have shuttered five of the state's six clinics. The Louisiana case was put on hold pending the outcome of Whole Woman's Health, and it was retried in light of the Supreme Court's judgement. While the District Court deemed the legislation unconstitutional, the Fifth Circuit determined that, unlike the Texas law, the burden of the Louisiana law passed the Whole Woman's Health standards, and hence the law was valid. The Supreme Court issued an order suspending the law's enforcement pending further review and agreed to hear the matter in its entirety in October 2019. It was the first abortion-related issue considered by the Court's new justices, Neil Gorsuch and Brett Kavanaugh, who was appointed by President Donald Trump. The Louisiana statute was deemed unlawful by the Supreme Court on the identical grounds as the Texas law, overturning the Fifth Circuit. Chief Justice John Roberts, who had dissented in Whole Woman's Health but joined in judgement to protect the court's respect for the previous decision, in that case, backed the decision.

Women's Health Organisation v. Dobbs
The Supreme Court's composition at the time of Dobbs
In May 2021, the Supreme Court granted certiorari in
Dobbs v. Jackson Women's Health Organization, a
case challenging the impact of Roe v. Wade in
preventing the implementation of a 2018 Mississippi
statute that prohibited all abortions beyond the first 15
weeks.

Dobbs heard oral arguments in December 2021, and a
ruling is likely by the close of the 2021-22 Supreme
Court session. Texas established one of the most
severe abortion laws in the country on September 1,
2021, prohibiting most operations beyond six weeks.

Politico reported on a leaked draft majority ruling in
this case on May 2, 2022. If such an opinion becomes
the court's formal majority opinion, it will overturn
Roe. If Roe is reversed, trigger laws in 13 states would
go into force, outlawing abortion.

On June 24, 2022, by a vote of 6-3, the Supreme Court
overturned both Roe v. Wade and Planned Parenthood
v. Casey in the Dobbs case, with the Chief Justice of
the United States concurring. Following the verdict,
abortion became illegal in certain states, and trigger
legislation in others would go into place shortly after.
Current legal situation
Federal regulations
Since 1995, the United States House of
Representatives and Senate have pushed multiple times
to prohibit the practice of intact dilation and extraction,
sometimes known as partial-birth abortion,
spearheaded by legislative Republicans. These laws

were enacted by large margins both times, but President Bill Clinton vetoed them in April 1996 and October 1997, citing a lack of health exceptions. Supporters of the measure in Congress claim that a health provision would render the law unconstitutional since the Doe v. Bolton ruling defined "health" in broad terms, justifying any reason for getting an abortion. Following attempts by Congress to overcome the vetoes were failed.

The Born-Alive Infants Protection Act of 2002 ("BAIPA") was adopted by an Act of Congress on August 5, 2002, and signed into law by George W. Bush. It defends the human rights of babies born following a botched abortion attempt. A "person, human being, kid, or individual" is defined as a "born-alive newborn." The term "born alive" refers to the complete expulsion of an infant at any stage of development that has a heartbeat, pulsation of the umbilical cord, breath, or voluntary muscle movement, regardless of whether the umbilical cord was cut or the expulsion was natural, induced labor, cesarean section, or induced abortion.

The House enacted the Partial-Birth Abortion Ban Act on October 2, 2003, by a vote of 281-142, to prohibit partial-birth abortion with an exemption in circumstances of fatal danger to the woman. A doctor who performs such surgery might face up to two years in jail and civil lawsuits under this legislation. Under the law, a woman undergoing the treatment could not be prosecuted. The measure was passed by the United States Senate on October 21, 2003, by a vote of 64-34, with a handful of Democrats joining in favour. President George W. Bush signed the measure on November 5, 2003, but a federal court stopped its implementation in certain states just hours later. On April 18, 2007, the Supreme Court upheld the countrywide prohibition on the operation in Gonzales v. Carhart, signifying a significant shift in the Court's approach to abortion legislation. The 5-4 judgment stated that the Partial-Birth Abortion Ban Act did not contradict earlier abortion decisions.

Following the Supreme Court of the United States' landmark judgment in Roe v. Wade in 1973, and later companion rulings, the judicial interpretation of the United States Constitution on abortion is that abortion is allowed but may be regulated to differing degrees by the states. States have passed legislation to limit late-term abortions, require parental notification for minors, and require abortion risk information to be disclosed to patients before the surgery.

Following extensive hearings on the Human Life Amendment (sponsored by Senators Orrin Hatch and Thomas Eagleton), the official report of the United States Senate Judiciary Committee, released in 1983, stated:

As a result, the Judiciary] Committee concludes that there are no substantial legal hurdles of any type in the United States today for a mother to get an abortion for any reason at any point of her pregnancy.

One part of the current legal abortion regime has been identifying when the fetus is "viable" outside the womb as a measure of when the fetus's "life" is its own (and therefore subject to being protected by the state). In the majority judgement in Roe v. Wade, the court defined viability as "Potentially capable of living outside of the mother's womb, although with artificial assistance. The average time for viability is seven months (28 weeks), however, it can occur sooner, even at 24 weeks ". When the court issued its decision in 1973, medical science at the time showed that viability may emerge as early as 24 weeks. Advances in the last three decades have allowed some babies delivered at 22 weeks to survive.

In 2006, the youngest child in the United States to survive a preterm delivery was a girl delivered at Kapiolani Medical Centre in Honolulu, Hawaii, at 21 weeks and 3 days gestation.

 Legal abortion availability varies by the state due to the divide between federal and state law. Geographic availability varies greatly, with no abortion provider in 87 percent of U.S. counties. Furthermore, many state health plans do not cover abortions owing to the Hyde Amendment; as of 2022, 17 states (including California, Illinois, and New York) offer or mandate such coverage.

Abortion is typically a prominent topic in nomination debates for the United States Supreme Court. Because the matter may come before them as judges, nominees often keep mute during their hearings.

The Unborn Victims of Violence Act, often known as "Laci and Conner's Law," was approved by Congress and signed into law by President Bush on April 1, 2004, making it possible to pursue two charges against someone who kills a pregnant woman (one for the mother and one for the foetus). It expressly prohibits accusations against the mother and/or doctor for abortion operations. Nonetheless, it has sparked much debate among pro-abortion rights campaigners, who see it as a potential step toward outlawing abortion. The Pain-Capable Unborn Child Protection Act is a United States Congress measure that would prohibit late-term abortions beyond 20 weeks of pregnancy on the grounds that the fetus is capable of feeling pain during and after the abortion. The measure was proposed in Congress for the first time in 2013. It was passed by the House of Representatives in 2013, 2015, and 2017, but it has yet to be passed by the Senate. Opponents of the law dispute the bill's backers' statements about foetal development and contend that such a limitation would jeopardise women's health.

Legal status varies by state.

States where the right to abortion is guaranteed by state legislation, a state supreme court judgment, or both.

State legislation protects abortion access.

The right to abortion is guaranteed under the state constitution.

Both state law and the state constitution preserve abortion access.

There are no state-level safeguards.

Articles of primary importance: Abortion in the United States, broken down by state Different types of abortion restrictions exist in the United States.

Prior to 2022, abortion was legal in every state in the United States, and each state had at least one abortion facility.

 Abortion is a contentious political subject, and most states strive to limit it on a regular basis. Two similar lawsuits, starting in Texas and Louisiana, resulted in the Supreme Court decisions Whole Woman's Health v. Hellerstedt (2016) and June Medical Services, LLC v. Russo (2020), which overturned many Texas and Louisiana limitations.

Minors and abortion are controlled at the state level, with 37 states requiring parental participation, either in the form of parental permission or parental notification. A court can override parental prohibitions in certain circumstances. Common abortion rules include obligatory waiting periods, ultrasounds, and scripted counseling. Abortion regulations in conservative Southern states are often tighter than in other areas of the country.

The Reproductive Health Act (RHA) of New York was approved in 2019, repealing a pre-Roe clause that prohibited third-trimester abortions except in circumstances when the continuation of the pregnancy risked a pregnant woman's life.

Abortion is banned in the Northern Mariana Islands, a United States Commonwealth territory.

On April 30, 2019, Alabama House Republicans passed legislation that, if implemented, will outlaw most abortions.

 The "Human Life Protection Act," as it is known, allows for just two exceptions: a major health danger

to the mother or a deadly foetal abnormality. Amendments that would have added rape and incest instances to the list of exclusions were defeated. The surgery will also be classified as a Class A felony. On May 13, twenty-five male Alabama senators voted to enact the measure. 0 The measure was signed into law the next day by Alabama Governor Kay Ivey, mostly as a symbolic gesture with the goal of challenging Roe v. Wade in the Supreme Court. 0 0
Since Alabama passed the first contemporary anti-abortion legislation in April 2019, five additional states, including Mississippi, Kentucky, Ohio, Georgia, and, most recently, Louisiana on May 30, 2019, have passed abortion laws.
0
In May 2019, the United States Supreme Court upheld an Indiana state statute requiring aborted foetuses to be buried or burned.
0 In a case decided in December 2019, the Supreme Court declined to hear an appeal of a lower court ruling upholding a Kentucky statute mandating doctors to do ultrasounds and reveal fetal pictures to patients before performing abortions. 0
On June 29, 2020, the United States Supreme Court seemed to uphold prior Supreme Court judgments against abortion restrictions when it knocked down the Louisiana anti-abortion statute.
0 Following the decision, the constitutionality of abortion restrictions in states such as Ohio was brought into doubt. 0 It was also observed that Supreme Court Chief Justice John Roberts, who agreed that the

Louisiana anti-abortion statute was unconstitutional, had previously voted to maintain a similar Texas law that was thrown down by the United States Supreme Court in 2016. 0

Texas lawmakers approved the Texas Heartbeat Act in May 2021, prohibiting abortions as soon as heart activity is found, commonly as early as six weeks into pregnancy, and frequently before women realize they are pregnant owing to the duration of the menstrual cycle (which usually lasts a median of four weeks and in some cases can be irregular).

0 To avoid traditional Roe v. Wade constitutional challenges, the law states that anyone, with or without a vested interest, may sue anyone who "performs or induces an abortion in violation of the statute," as well as anyone who "aids or abets the performance or inducement of an abortion, including paying for or reimbursing the costs of an abortion through insurance or otherwise."The law was challenged in court, but it had yet to receive a full official hearing as its enactment date of September 1, 2021, approached. Plaintiffs requested an injunction from the United States Supreme Court to prevent the legislation from taking effect, but the Court denied the request late on September 1, 2021, allowing the statute to stay in place. While unsigned, Chief Justice John Roberts and Justice Stephen Breyer authored dissenting views, which were supported by Justices Elena Kagan and Sonia Sotomayor, which would have given an injunction on the statute until a proper judicial review could be conducted.1

Attorney General Merrick Garland, the head of the United States Department of Justice, sued the State of Texas over the Texas Act on September 9, 2021, claiming that "the law is invalid under the Supremacy Clause and the Fourteenth Amendment, is preempted by federal law and violates the doctrine of intergovernmental immunity."

1 Garland went on to say that the US government has a "responsibility to guarantee that no state can strip persons of their constitutional rights."According to the Complaint, Texas passed the bill "in flagrant contempt of the Constitution."The relief sought from the United States District Court for the District of Texas in Austin includes a determination that the Texas Act is unconstitutional, as well as an injunction against state actors and any and all private people who may initiate an SB 8 case.1 It is unusual and has raised eyebrows to petition a federal court to impose an injunction on a state's whole civilian population.1

In contrast, Colorado approved the Reproductive Health Equity Act in April 2022, which guarantees abortion access to all state residents. While the bill as it was passed maintained the status quo for abortion rights, it guarantees that "every individual has a fundamental right to make decisions about the individual's reproductive health care, including the fundamental right to use or refuse contraception; a pregnant individual has a fundamental right to continue a pregnancy and give birth or to have an abortion and to make decisions about how to exercise that right; and a fertilized egg, embryo, or fetus does not have a fundamental right to life".1

A variety of additional variables are thought to have contributed to the emergence of anti-abortion legislation. Physicians, who were among the most vocal supporters of abortion-criminalization legislation, appear to have been motivated in part by breakthroughs in medical knowledge. Science had found that conception began a more or less continuous process of development that resulted in the birth of a new human being. Quickening was discovered to be neither more nor less important than any other phase in the gestation process. Many doctors reasoned that if society thought it was unreasonable to terminate a pregnancy after the foetus had quickened, and if quickening was a relatively inconsequential phase in the gestation process, then terminating a pregnancy before quickening was just as wrong. Ideologically, the Hippocratic Oath and the medical mentality of the time in defending the absolute dignity of human life had a key impact in shaping ideas regarding abortion. Doctors were also driven by practical considerations to lobby for anti-abortion legislation. For one thing, abortion providers tended to be inexperienced and unaffiliated with medical groups. In an era when the nation's top doctors were seeking to standardise the medical profession, these "irregulars" were viewed as a threat to public health. The "irregulars" were resented by the more structured medical profession because they were competitors, typically at a lower cost.

Despite anti-abortion initiatives, abortifacient advertising was very effective, and abortion was widely practiced in the mid-nineteenth century. While the exact abortion percentage remained unknown, James Mohr's 1978 book Abortion in America uncovered various published estimations by 19th-century physicians that claimed that between 15% and 35% of all pregnancies terminated in abortion during that time period. This era also saw a significant shift in the number of persons getting abortions. Prior to the turn of the century, most abortions were obtained by unmarried women who had fallen pregnant outside of marriage. More than half of the 54 abortion cases published in American medical journals between 1839 and 1880 were sought by married women, and more than 60% of the married women already had at least one child. Many conservative physicians, almost mostly males, were concerned that married women were increasingly seeking abortions. During the Reconstruction period, the emerging women's rights movement bore a large share of the responsibility. Though the medical profession was hostile to feminism, many feminists of the time were also anti-abortion.

 An editorial piece was published in the publication The Revolution, which was run by Elizabeth Cady Stanton and Susan B. Anthony, stating that rather than simply trying to establish legislation prohibiting abortion, the main problem must also be addressed. According to the author, simply establishing an anti-abortion law would be sufficient "be merely mowing off the top of the poisonous weed while the root remains... No matter what the purpose, love of ease, or a wish to rescue the unborn innocent from suffering, the woman who performs the action is dreadfully guilty. It would burden her conscience in life and her soul in death; but oh! he is threefold guilty of driving her to the desperation that drove her to the crime." Many feminists of the time saw abortion as an unwelcome need imposed on women by foolish males.

 Even the feminist movement's "free love" wing refused to push for abortion, viewing it as an indication of the horrible extremes to which contemporary marriage was forcing women. Marital rape and unmarried women's seduction were societal evils that feminists blamed for the need to abort since males did not respect women's right to abstinence.

Physicians, on the other hand, were the most outspoken opponents of abortion, taking their cause to state legislatures across the country, demanding not only anti-abortion legislation but also legislation against birth control. This campaign foreshadowed today's controversy over women's body rights. A campaign was developed to oppose the trend, as well as the usage and availability of contraception. Abortion became illegal in the late 1860s, thanks to the efforts of concerned politicians, doctors, and the American Medical Association.

 Anthony Comstock founded the New York Society for the Suppression of Vice in 1873, an organisation committed to monitoring public morals. Later the same year, Comstock successfully lobbied the United States

Congress to adopt the Comstock Law, which made it illegal to send "obscene, vulgar, or lascivious" literature through the United States mail. It also outlawed the production or distribution of material relevant to the procurement of abortion, the prevention of conception, or the transmission of venereal disease, even to medical students. The Comstock Law prohibited the creation, publishing, importation, and dissemination of such items as obscene, and equivalent laws were enacted by 24 of the 37 states.

Abortion was a crime in every state in 1900. Some states contained abortion provisions, primarily to safeguard the woman's life or to terminate pregnancies resulting from rape or incest. Abortions, on the other hand, continued to occur and grew more widely available. Margaret Sanger created the American Birth Control League in 1921, which later became the Planned Parenthood Federation of America in 1942.

By the 1930s, licensed doctors were performing an estimated 800,000 abortions every year.

Finkbine, Sherri

Sherri Chessen is the main article.

A scandal centered on children's television show Sherri Finkbine in the early 1960s helped push abortion and abortion law more squarely into the American public spotlight. Finkbine had four healthy children while living in Phoenix, Arizona, but during her fifth pregnancy, she realised the kid would be born with serious defects. This was most likely due to Finkbine's usage of sleeping medications that included thalidomide, a medicine that raises the risk of congenital abnormalities during pregnancy. Finkbine desired an abortion, but Arizona abortion regulations prohibited abortions unless the woman's life was in danger. The tale went viral after Finkbine told it to a writer from The Arizona Republic, who revealed her identity despite her demands for anonymity. Finkbine proceeded to Sweden on August 18, 1962, to get a legal abortion, when it was discovered that the fetus had significant malformations. Finkbine's tale was a watershed moment in the history of women's reproductive rights and abortion law in the United States. Still, Finkbine was only able to receive an abortion because she could afford to fly overseas for it, underscoring a continuing imbalance in abortion rights in which many women cannot pay or otherwise do not have the ability to seek a legal abortion. In such instances, women may resort to illegal abortion methods.

Precedents Prior to Roe

Gerri Santoro of Connecticut died in 1964 while attempting to undergo an illegal abortion, and her photograph became a symbol of the abortion-rights movement. Some women's rights activists acquired their own talents in order to deliver abortions to women who couldn't get them elsewhere. In Chicago, for example, a group known as "Jane" ran a floating abortion clinic for most of the 1960s. Women interested in the procedure would dial a certain number and be directed to "Jane."

The United States Supreme Court decision Griswold v. Connecticut in 1965 overturned one of the last surviving contraceptive Comstock statutes in Connecticut and Massachusetts.

 Griswold, on the other hand, exclusively extended to marital partnerships, enabling married couples to purchase and use contraception without government intervention. It took until 1972, in Eisenstadt v. Baird, to extend the Griswold precedent to unmarried people as well. Following the Griswold case, the American College of Obstetricians and Gynaecologists (ACOG) issued a medical bulletin accepting a six-year-old recommendation that clarified that "conception is the implantation of a fertilised ovum," and birth control methods that prevented implantation were classified as contraceptives rather than abortifacients.

Colorado was the first state to legalize abortion in circumstances of rape, incest, or pregnancy that would result in the woman's irreversible physical handicap. Similar legislation has been enacted in California, Oregon, and North Carolina. In 1970, Hawaii became the first state to decriminalize abortion on the woman's request, while New York abolished its 1830 legislation, allowing abortions up to the 24th week of pregnancy. Similar legislation was quickly enacted in Alaska and Washington. Washington conducted a referendum on legalizing early pregnancy abortions in 1970, becoming the first state to do so by popular vote.

 In the United States v. Vuitch, the Supreme Court upheld the legislation in Washington, D.C. that permitted abortion to preserve a woman's life or health. The bill was affirmed by the court, which determined that "health" encompassed "psychological and physical well-being," thereby legalizing abortion in Washington, D.C. By the end of 1972, 13 states had laws comparable to Colorado's, with Mississippi allowing abortion only in situations of rape or incest, and Alabama and Massachusetts allowing abortions only when the woman's physical health was jeopardized. During this time, women would frequently travel from a state where abortion was prohibited to one where it was permitted to receive abortions. Prior to Roe v. Wade, abortion was prohibited in 30 states and permissible under limited conditions in the remaining 20.

In the late 1960s, a number of groups were founded to organize public opinion both for and against abortion legalization. Monsignor James T. McHugh was tasked by the National Conference of Catholic Bishops in 1966 to chronicle attempts to modify abortion legislation, and anti-abortion groups began to develop in several states in 1967. McHugh headed an advisory committee that became the National Right to Life Committee in 1968. The NARAL Pro-Choice America was founded in 1969 to oppose abortion restrictions and to increase access to abortion.

 Following Roe v. Wade, NARAL renamed itself the National Abortion Rights Action League in late 1973. On May 25, 2022, Oklahoma imposed a ban on elective abortions after Oklahoma Governor Kevin Stitt signed House Bill 4327. The bill bans elective abortion beginning at conception.The law also permits private citizens to file lawsuits against abortion providers who knowingly provide, perform, or induce elective abortions on a pregnant woman. Abortion in cases of rape, incest, or high-risk pregnancies continues to be permitted.A lawsuit was immediately filed by the ACLU in opposition to the bill2Currently, Oklahoma is the only U.S. state to pass a bill imposing such restrictions, and, should the bill remain in effect, it will become the first U.S. state to ban elective abortion procedures since prior to the ruling and implementation of Roe v. Wade in 1973. 2 21

After the Supreme Court overturned Roe v. Wade on June 24, 2022, Texas and Missouri immediately banned abortions with exceptions only for rape and incest.

In response to the coronavirus pandemic

Main article: Impact of the COVID-19 pandemic on abortion in the United States

Amid the COVID-19 pandemic, anti-abortion government officials in several American states enacted or attempted to enact restrictions on abortion, characterizing it as a non-essential procedure that can be suspended during a medical emergency.

2 The orders have led to several legal challenges and criticism by human rights groups and several national medical organizations, including the American Medical Association.Legal challenges on behalf of abortion providers, many of which are represented by the American Civil Liberties Union and Planned Parenthood, have successfully stopped most of the orders on a temporary basis. 2

One challenge was made against the FDA's rule on the distribution of mifepristone (RU-486), one of the two-part drug regimens to induce abortions. Since 2000, it has only been available through health providers under the FDA's ruling. Due to the COVID-19 pandemic, access to mifepristone was a concern, and the American College of Obstetricians and Gynecologists along with other groups sued to have the rule relaxed to allow women to be able to access mifepristone at home through mail-order or retail pharmacies. While the Fourth Circuit issued a preliminary injunction against the FDA's ruling that would have allowed wider distribution, the Supreme Court ordered in a 6–3 decision in January 2021 to put a stay on the injunction, maintaining the FDA's rule. 2

Sanctuary city for the unborn

Since 2019, the anti-abortion movement in the United States has been pushing for anti-abortion rules such as declarations of "sanctuary city for the unborn".

2 In June 2019, the city council of Waskom, Texas, voted to outlaw abortion in the city, declaring Waskom a "sanctuary city for the unborn" (the first such city to designate itself as such), as state governments elsewhere in the United States also were drafting abortion bans.3 As of June–July 2019, there is no abortion clinic in the city.3 The Waskom ordinance has led other small cities in Texas, and as of April 2021 in Nebraska, to vote in favor of becoming "sanctuary cities for the unborn".33

On April 6, 2021, Hayes Center, Nebraska, became the first city in Nebraska to outlaw abortion by local ordinance, declaring itself a "sanctuary city for the unborn."

3 The city of Blue Hill, Nebraska, followed suit and enacted a similar ordinance outlawing abortion on April 13, 2021.3 In May 2021, Lubbock, Texas, with a population of less than 270,000, voted to become the largest city in the U.S. to ban abortion with the "sanctuary city for the unborn ordinance".

Abortion financing

See the link in the caption for a text equivalent

State Medicaid coverage of medically necessary abortion services (text-based list):

   Medicaid covers medically necessary abortion for low-income women through legislation.

   Medicaid covers medically necessary abortions for low-income women under court order.

   Medicaid denies abortion coverage for low-income women except for cases of rape, incest, or life endangerment.

The abortion debate has also been extended to the question of who pays the medical costs of the procedure, with some states using the mechanism as a way of reducing the number of abortions.

The cost of an abortion varies depending on factors such as location, facility, timing, and type of procedure. In 2005, a non-hospital abortion at 10 weeks' gestation ranged from $90 to $1,800 (average: $430), whereas an abortion at 20 weeks' gestation ranged from $350 to $4,520 (average: $1,260). citation needed] Costs are higher for a medical abortion than a first-trimester surgical abortion. citation needed] A variety of resources from support organisations are available to contribute to the costs of the procedure, as well as travel expenses.

Abortion fund organizations

A variety of organizations offer financial support for people seeking abortions, including travel and other expenses.

Access Reproductive Care–Southeast (ARC Southeast), the Brigid Alliance, the Midwest Access Coalition (MAC), and the National Network of Abortion Funds are examples of such groups.

Medicaid

The Hyde Amendment is a federal legislative provision barring the use of federal Medicaid funds to pay for abortions except for rape and incest.

The provision, in various forms, was in response to Roe v. Wade, has been routinely attached to annual appropriations bills since 1976, and represented the first major legislative success by the pro-life movement. The law requires that states cover abortions under Medicaid in the event of rape, incest, and life endangerment. Based on the federal law:

32 states and D.C. fund abortions through Medicaid only in the cases of rape, incest, or life endangerment.

SD covers abortions only in the cases of life endangerment, which does not comply with federal requirements under the Hyde Amendment. IN, UT, and WI have expanded coverage to women whose physical health is jeopardised, and IA, MS, UT, and VA also include foetal abnormality cases.

17 states (AK, AZ, CA, CT, HI, IL, MD, MA, MN, MT, NJ, NM, NY, OR, VT, WA, WV) use their own

funds to cover all or most "medically necessary" abortions sought by low-income women under Medicaid, 12 of which are required by State court orders to do so.

Private insurance

5 states (ID, KY, MO, ND, OK) restrict insurance coverage of abortion services in private plans: OK limits coverage to life endangerment, rape, or incest circumstances; and the other four states limit coverage to cases of life endangerment.

11 states (CO, KY, MA, MS, NE, ND, OH, PA, RI, SC, VA) restrict abortion coverage in insurance plans for public employees, with CO and KY restricting insurance coverage of abortion under any circumstances.

U.S. laws also ban federal funding of abortions for federal employees and their dependents, Native Americans covered by the Indian Health Service, military personnel and their dependents, and women with disabilities covered by Medicare.

Mexico City policy

Main article: Mexico City policy

Under this policy, U.S. federal funding to NGOs that provide abortion is not permitted.

Qualifying requirements for abortion providers

Qualifying requirements for performing abortions vary from state to state, and are since 2019 been changed in several states by lawmakers who anticipate the possibility that Roe v. Wade may soon be overturned.

As of 2019, New York, Illinois,5 as well as Maine,5 allow non-physician health professionals, such as physician assistants, nurse practitioners, and certified nurse midwives, to act within their scope of practice, to perform abortion procedures; their laws do not explicitly specify which types of abortions these non-physicians may do. California, Oregon, Montana, Vermont, and New Hampshire allow qualified non-physician health professionals to do first-trimester aspiration abortions and to prescribe drugs for medical abortions. Washington State, New Mexico, Alaska, Maryland, Massachusetts, Connecticut, and New Jersey allow qualified non-physicians to prescribe drugs for medical abortions only.(Maryland has passed legislation which will allow qualified non-physician health professionals to do abortion procedures in clinics, early in pregnancy, beginning July 1, 2022. 5) In all other states, only licensed physicians may perform abortions.In 2016, the FDA issued new guidelines recommending that qualified non-physician healthcare professionals be allowed to prescribe mifepristone in all states; however, these guidelines are not binding, and states are free to determine their own policies regarding mifepristone. 5

Number of abortions

The annual number of legal induced abortions in the U.S. doubled between 1973 and 1979 and peaked in 1990. There was a slow but steady decline throughout the 1990s. Overall, the number of annual abortions decreased by 6% between 2000 and 2009, with temporary spikes in 2002 and 2006. 6

By 2011, the abortion rate in the nation dropped to its lowest point since the Supreme Court legalized the procedure. According to a study performed by Guttmacher Institute, long-acting contraceptive methods had a significant impact on reducing unwanted pregnancies. There were fewer than 17 abortions for every 1,000 women of child-bearing age. That was a 13%-decrease from 2008's numbers and slightly higher than the rate in 1973 when the Supreme Court's Roe v. Wade decision legalized abortion. 6 The study indicated a long-term decline in the abortion rate. 6 6 6

In 2016, the Centers for Disease Control and Prevention (CDC) reported 623,471 abortions, a 2% decrease from 636,902 in 2015.

6

Medical abortions

A Guttmacher Institute survey of abortion providers estimated that early medical abortions accounted for 17% of all non-hospital abortions and slightly over one-quarter of abortions before 9 weeks gestation in the United States in 2008.

6 Medical abortions were voluntarily reported to the CDC by 34 reporting areas (excluding Alabama, California, Connecticut, Delaware, Florida, Hawaii, Illinois, Louisiana, Maryland, Massachusetts, Nebraska, Nevada, New Hampshire, Pennsylvania, Tennessee, Vermont, Wisconsin, and Wyoming) and published in its annual abortion surveillance reports have increased every year since the September 28, 2000, FDA approval of mifepristone (RU-486): 1.0% in 2000, 2.9% in 2001, 5.2% in 2002, 7.9% in 2003, 9.3% in 2004, 9.9% in 2005, 10.6% in 2006, 13.1% in

2007, 15.8% in 2008, 17.1% in 2009 (25.2% of those at less than 9 weeks gestation). 6 Medical abortions accounted for 32% of first-trimester abortions at Planned Parenthood clinics in 2008. 6

Abortion and religion

A majority of abortions are obtained by religiously identified women. According to the Guttmacher Institute, "more than 7 in 10 U.S. women obtaining an abortion report a religious affiliation (37% protestant, 28% Catholic, and 7% other), and 25% attend religious services at least once a month. The abortion rate for protestant women is 15 per 1,000 women, while Catholic women have a slightly higher rate, 20 per 1,000." 6

Abortions and ethnicity

Abortion rates tend to be higher among minority women in the U.S. In 2000–2001, the rates among black and Hispanic women were 49 per 1,000 and 33 per 1,000, respectively, vs. 13 per 1,000 among non-Hispanic white women. Note that this figure includes all women of reproductive age, including women that are not pregnant. In other words, these abortion rates reflect the rate at which U.S. women of reproductive age have an abortion each year.

In 2004, the rates of abortion by ethnicity in the U.S. were 50 abortions per 1,000 black women, 28 abortions per 1,000 Hispanic women, and 11 abortions per 1,000 white women.

77

REASONS FOR ABORTION

A 1998 study revealed that from 1987 to 1988, women reported the following as their primary reasons for choosing an abortion:
77
25.5%   Want to postpone childbearing
21.3%   Cannot afford a baby
14.1%   Has relationship problems or partner does not want pregnancy
12.2%
Too young; parent(s) or other(s) object to pregnancy
10.8%
Having a child will disrupt education or employment
7.9%   Want no (more) children
3.3%   Risk to foetal health
When women have abortions (by gestational age)
Abortion in the U.S. by gestational age, 20167
According to the Centers for Disease Control, in 2011, most (64.5%) abortions were performed by ≤8 weeks' gestation, and nearly all (91.4%) were performed by <13 weeks' gestation. Few abortions (7.3%) were performed between 14 and 20 weeks gestation or at ≥21 weeks' gestation (1.4%). From 2002 to 2011, the percentage of all abortions performed at ≤8 weeks' gestation increased by 6%. 7
Safety of abortions
: Abortion § Safety
The risk of death from carrying a child to term in the U.S. is approximately 14 times greater than the risk of death from a legal abortion.

The risk of abortion-related mortality increases with gestational age but remains lower than that of childbirth through at least 21 weeks of gestation.
Birth control effects
Main article: Birth control
Increased access to birth control has been statistically linked to reductions in the abortion rate.
As an element of family planning, birth control was federally subsidised for low-income families in 1965 under President Lyndon B. Johnson's War on Poverty program. In 1970, Congress passed Title X to provide family planning services for those in need, and President Richard Nixon signed it into law. Funding for Title X rose from $6 million in 1971 to $61 million the next year, and slowly increased each year to $317 million in 2010, after which it was reduced by a few percent.
In 2011, the Guttmacher Institute reported that the number of abortions in the U.S. would be nearly two-thirds higher without access to birth control.
 In 2015, the Federation of American Scientists reported that federally mandated access to birth control had helped reduce teenage pregnancies in the U.S. by 44 percent, and had prevented more than 188,000 unintended pregnancies.

CHAPTER 3

Public opinion

Americans have been equally divided on the issue; a May 2018 Gallup poll indicated that 48% of Americans described themselves as "pro-choice" and 48% described themselves as "pro-life".

 A July 2018 poll indicated that 64% of Americans did not want the Supreme Court to overturn Roe v. Wade, while 28% did. 8 The same poll found that support for abortion is generally legal was 60% during the first trimester, dropping to 28% in the second trimester, and 13% in the third trimester. 8

Support for the legalization of abortion has been consistently higher among more educated adults than less educated,8 and in 2019, 70% of college graduates support abortion being legal in all or most cases, compared to 60% of those with some college, and 54% of those with a high school degree or less.

In January 2013, a majority of Americans believed abortion should be legal in all or most cases, according to a poll by NBC News and The Wall Street Journal.

 Approximately 70% of respondents in the same poll opposed Roe v. Wade being overturned. A poll by the Pew Research Centre yielded similar results. 9

Moreover, 48% of Republicans opposed overturning Roe, compared to 46% who supported overturning it. Gallup declared in May 2010 that more Americans identifying as "pro-life" is "the new normal", while also noting that there had been no increase in opposition to abortion. It suggested that political polarization may have prompted more Republicans to call themselves "pro-life". The terms "pro-choice" and "pro-life" do not always reflect a political view or fall along a binary; in one Public Religion Research Institute poll, seven in ten Americans described themselves as "pro-choice" while almost two-thirds described themselves as "pro-life". The same poll found that 56% of Americans were in favor of legal access to abortion in all or some cases.

A 2022 study reviewing the literature and public opinion datasets found that 43.8% of survey respondents in the U.S. consistently support both elective and traumatic abortion, whereas only 14.8% consistently oppose abortion irrespective of the reason, and others differ in their degree of support for abortion depending on the circumstances of the abortion.

 90% approve of abortion when the health of the woman is endangered, 77.4% when there is a strong chance of defects in the baby that could result from the pregnancy and 79.5% when the pregnancy is the result of rape.

By gender and age

Pew Research Centre polling shows little change in views from 2008 to 2012; modest differences based on gender or age.

The original article's table also shows party affiliation, religion, and education level.

By educational level

Support for the legalization of abortion is significantly higher among more educated adults than less educated and has been consistently so for decades.

 In 2019, 70% of college graduates support abortion being legal in all or most cases, as well as 60% of those with some college education, compared to 54% of those with a high school degree or less

By gender, party, and region

A January 2003 CBS News/The New York Times poll examined whether Americans thought abortion should be legal or not and found variations in an opinion that depended upon party affiliation and the region of the country.

The margin of error is +/– 4% for questions answered by the entire sample (overall figures) and may be higher for questions asked of subgroups (all other figures).

By the trimester of pregnancy

A CNN/USA Today/Gallup poll in January 2003 asked about the legality of abortion by trimester, using the question, "Do you think abortion should generally be legal or generally illegal during each of the following stages of pregnancy?"

This same question was also asked by Gallup in March 2000 and July 1996. 9 9 Polls indicate general support for legal abortion during the first trimester, although support drops dramatically for abortion during the second and third trimesters.

By circumstance or reasons

According to Gallup's long-time polling on abortion, the majority of Americans are neither strictly "pro-life" nor "pro-choice"; it depends upon the circumstances of the pregnancy. Gallup polling from 1996 to 2021 consistently reveals that when asked the question, "Do you think abortions should be legal under any circumstances, legal only under certain circumstances, or illegal in all circumstances?", Americans repeatedly answer "legal only under certain circumstances". According to the poll, in any given year 48–57% say legal only under certain circumstances, 21–34% say legal under any circumstances, and 13–19% illegal in all circumstances, with 1–7% having no opinion. Since the 2011 poll, support for legal abortion during the first trimester has declined.

According to the aforementioned poll,9 Americans differ drastically based on the situation of the pregnancy, suggesting they do not support unconditional abortions. Based on two separate polls taken May 19–21, 2003, of 505 and 509 respondents respectively, Americans stated their approval for abortion under these various circumstances:

Poll Criteria	Total	Poll A	Poll B
When the woman's life is endangered	78%	82%	75%
When the pregnancy was caused by rape	65%	72%	59%
When the child would be born with an illness	54%	60%	48%

When the child would be born mentally
disabled   44%   50%   38%
When the woman does not want the child for any
reason   32%
Additional polls
Results of Gallup opinion poll in the U.S. since 1975,
legal restriction of abortion
A June 2000 Los Angeles Times survey found that,
although 57% of poll takers considered abortion to be
murder, half of that 57% believed in allowing women
access to abortion. The survey also found that, overall,
65% of respondents did not believe abortion should be
legal after the first trimester, including 72% of women
and 58% of men. Further, the survey found that 85% of
Americans polled supported abortion in cases of risk to
a woman's physical health, 54% if the woman's mental
health was at risk, and 66% if a congenital abnormality
was detected in the fetus. 9
A July 2002 Public Agenda poll found that 44% of
men and 42% of women thought that "abortion should
be generally available to those who want it", 34% of
men and 35% of women thought that "abortion should
be available, but under stricter than limits it is now",
and 21% of men and 22% of women thought that
"abortion should not be permitted".
A January 2003 ABC News/The Washington Post poll
also examined attitudes towards abortion by gender. In
answer to the question, "On the subject of abortion, do
you think abortion should be legal in all cases, legal in
most cases, illegal in most cases, or illegal in all
cases?"25% of women responded that it should be

legal in "all cases", 33% that it should be legal in "most cases", 23% that it should be illegal in "most cases", and 17% that it should be illegal in "all cases". 20% of men thought it should be legal in "all cases", 34% legal in "most cases", 27% illegal in "most cases", and 17% illegal in "all cases". 0

Most Fox News viewers favor both parental notifications as well as parental consent when a minor seeks an abortion. A Fox News poll in 2005 found that 78% of people favour a notification requirement, and 72% favour a consent requirement.

An April 2006 Harris poll on Roe v. Wade, asked, "In 1973, the U.S. Supreme Court decided that states' laws which made it illegal for a woman to have an abortion up to three months of pregnancy were unconstitutional and that the decision on whether a woman should have an abortion up to three months of pregnancy should be left to the woman and her doctor to decide. In general, do you favor or oppose this part of the U.S. Supreme Court decision making abortions up to three months of pregnancy legal?", to which 49% of respondents indicated favor while 47% indicated opposition. The Harris organisation has concluded from this poll that, "49 percent now support Roe vs. Wade".

Two polls were released in May 2007 asking Americans "With respect to the abortion issue, would you consider yourself to be pro-choice or pro-life?" May 4–6, a CNN poll found that 45% said "pro-choice" and 50% said pro-life. Within the following week, a Gallup poll found 50% responding "pro-choice" and 44% pro-life.

In 2011, a poll conducted by the Public Religion Research Institute found that 43% of respondents identified themselves as both "pro-life" and "pro-choice".

Intact dilation and extraction

Further information: Intact dilation and extraction

: Partial-Birth Abortion Ban Act

In 2003, the U.S. Congress outlawed intact dilation and extraction when it passed the Partial-Birth Abortion Ban Act. A Rasmussen Reports poll four days after the Supreme Court's opinion in Gonzales v. Carhart found that 40% of respondents "knew the ruling allowed states to place some restrictions on specific abortion procedures." Of those who knew of the decision, 56% agreed with the decision, and 32% were opposed.An ABC poll from 2003 found that 62% of respondents thought partial-birth abortion should be illegal; a similar number of respondents wanted an exception "if it would prevent a serious threat to the woman's health".

Gallup has repeatedly queried the American public on this issue.

Positions of political parties in the United States

Though members of both main political parties can be found on either side of the abortion debate, the Republican Party is often seen as anti-abortion since the official party platform opposes abortion and believes that fetuses have an intrinsic right to life. Republicans for Choice represent the party's minority. In 2006, surveyors discovered that percent of Republicans support abortion access in most cases. In

2004, 13% of Republican National Convention delegates thought abortion should be widely available, while 38% said it should be illegal. According to the same study, 17 percent of all Republican voters say abortion should be available to anybody who wants it, while 38 percent feel it should not be authorized. Before their 1976 convention, the Republican Party supported an anti-abortion constitutional amendment as a temporary political ploy to gain more Catholic support, though this stance brought many more social conservatives into the party, resulting in a large and permanent shift toward support of the anti-abortion position.

Abortion is a woman's right, according to the Democratic Party platform. Democrats for Life of America represents the party's minority. Pollsters discovered in 2006 that 74% of Democrats support the availability of abortion in most situations. 0 In 2004, 75% of Democratic National Convention delegates agreed that abortion should be widely available, while 2% believed that abortion should be prohibited. According to the same study, 49 percent of all Democratic voters say abortion should be available to anybody who wants it, while 13 percent feel it should be illegal. 1

The United States Green Party believes that legal abortion is a woman's right. According to the Libertarian Party platform (2012), "government should be left out of the topic, leaving the question to each individual for conscientious thought."Abortion is a divisive subject among Libertarians, and the

Maryland-based organization Libertarians for Life opposes abortion legalization in most cases.
Abortion has become a highly contentious subject. In 2002, 84 percent of state Democratic platforms supported abortion rights, while 88 percent of state Republican platforms opposed them. This schism also resulted in Christian rights organisations such as Christian Voice, Christian Coalition, and Moral Majority playing a growing role in the Republican Party. This opposition has been extended under the Foreign Assistance Act: Jesse Helms introduced an amendment in 1973 prohibiting the use of aid money to promote abortion overseas, and the Mexico City policy in 1984 prohibited financial support to any overseas organization that performed or promoted abortions. President Bill Clinton withdrew the policy, which was later reintroduced by President George W. Bush. President Barack Obama reversed this policy by Executive Order on January 23, 2009,citation needed], and President Donald Trump reinstated it on January 23, 2017. On January 28, 2021, President Joe Biden signed a Presidential Memorandum repealing the restoration of Mexico City policy and directing the US Department of Health and Human Services to "suspend, rescind, or revoke" Title X limitations. 1 Legalisation's Consequences
Ms.'s winter 2013 issue focused on abortion rights. Because of enhanced physician abilities, greater medical technology, and early pregnancy termination, the risk of mortality from legal abortion has decreased significantly since its legalization in 1973.

1 From 1940 to 1970, the number of pregnant women killed during abortion decreased from roughly 1,500 to a little over 100.According to the Centers for Disease Control and Prevention, 39 women died in 1972 as a result of illegal abortion.The Roe effect is a concept that suggests that because advocates of abortion rights cause the loss of their political base by having fewer children, abortion will eventually be restricted or illegalized.Another contentious idea is the legalized abortion and crime impact, which contends that legalized abortion decreases crime because undesired offspring are more likely to become criminals.1 1 There have been various attempts to overturn Roe v. Wade since the judgement.

 Mississippi placed an amendment on the ballot during the 2011 election season that altered how the state regarded abortion. The personhood amendment defined personhood as "every human being from the time of conception, cloning, or the functional equivalent thereof"; if enacted, abortion in the state would have been banned.On July 11, 2012, a federal court in Mississippi extended his interim order to allow the state's only abortion facility to remain operational. The injunction was to remain in effect until U.S. District Judge Daniel Porter Jordan III could evaluate newly drafted guidelines governing how the Mississippi Department of Health would implement a new abortion statute. The relevant legislation went into force on July 1, 2012.

The Turnaway Study tracked a group of 1,000 women, two of whom died after giving birth,for five years after they sought an abortion, and contrasted the health and socioeconomic implications of getting or being denied an abortion.

According to the study, individuals who were supplied with abortion did better, while those who were refused one had unfavorable results.

Scientific Americans regarded it as a landmark.

If Roe v. Wade is overturned and abortion restrictions are imposed in trigger law states and states deemed extremely likely to outlaw abortion, "increases in travel distance are anticipated to prevent 93,546 to 143,561 women from receiving abortion treatment," according to a 2019 research.

 For the Dobbs v. Jackson Women's Health Organization case, which according to May 2022 leaks obtained by Politico is likely to overturn both Roe and Planned Parenthood v. Casey,2 among the over 130 amici curiae briefs, hundreds of scientists provided evidence, data, and studies, particularly the Turnaway Study, in support of abortion rights and to refute arguments made to the Court that abortion "has no beneficial effect on women's lives and careers—The final choice is scheduled to be made in late June or early July 2022.A follow-up Turnaway Study has been announced to determine the health and economic consequences if Roe is upheld.

Unwanted live birth

Even though it is uncommon, women do give birth despite an attempted abortion.

Although reporting of live births following attempted abortion varies by state, 38 were documented in one research in upstate New York two-and-a-half years before Roe v. Wade.The Born-Alive Infants Protection Act of 2002 requires medical personnel to report a live birth if they observe any breathing, heartbeat, umbilical cord pulsation, or confirmed voluntary muscle movement, regardless of whether the born-alive is non-viable ex utero in the long term due to birth defects, and regardless of gestational age, including gestational ages that are too early for long-term viability ex utero.

Background

In 2013, North Dakota became the first state to pass legislation banning abortions after six weeks. In 2015, the law was ruled unconstitutional under the precedent set by the U.S. Supreme Court decision Roe v. Wade (1973). Eleven states have proposed bills for six-week abortion bans since 2018; since 2019, such bills have passed including bills in Ohio, Georgia, Louisiana, Missouri, Alabama, Kentucky, South Carolina, and Texas, most of which lie either partly or entirely in the Bible Belt. Utah and Arkansas voted to limit the procedure to the middle of the second trimester. As of June 2021, except for the Texas bill, none of the laws are in effect due to court intervention.   The Guttmacher Institute writes that "state policymakers are testing the limits of what the new U.S. Supreme Court majority might allow and laying the groundwork for a day when federal constitutional protections for abortion are weakened or eliminated entirely." Texas has taken a novel approach in their wording of the legislation; rather than have the government enforce the law, private citizens are to be allowed to sue the provider or anyone that helps the woman to get an abortion. The Texas Tribune writes that "supporters of the bill hope this novel provision will trip up legal challenges to the legislation, as without state officials enforcing the ban, there will be nobody for pro-women's rights groups to sue."

Timing

Because the start of pregnancy is measured from the date of a woman's last menstruation (generally about two weeks before conception), six weeks into a pregnancy equals four weeks of embryonic development, and only two weeks after a woman's first missed period, when many women are unaware that they are pregnant.

 Most women who have an abortion do so after six weeks' gestation. Reproductive rights advocates contend that because of these and other reasons, the "fetal heartbeat bills" are de facto bans on abortion.

Terminology

While some of these laws ban abortions after six weeks of pregnancy and are called "fetal heartbeat" laws by their proponents who claim that a fetal heartbeat can be detected at six weeks, doctors have said that the term "fetal heartbeat" at that stage is false and intentionally misleading.

 A conceptus is not called a foetus until after ten weeks of pregnancy, before which the proper term is an embryo. Additionally, at six weeks the embryo has no heart, only a group of cells that will become a heart, calling it a heartbeat is also misleading. The heart will only have formed enough to be able to hear a real foetal heartbeat by 17–20 weeks of gestation. Jennifer Keats, an OB-GYN at the University of California, San Francisco, stated that the embryo's cardiovascular system at six weeks is "very immature". Keats described the cardiac activity as "a group of cells with electrical activity. That's what the heartbeat is at that stage of gestation ... We are in no way talking about any kind of cardiovascular system."

Ted Anderson, formerly president of the American College of Obstetricians and Gynecologists (ACOG), said that "ACOG does not use the term 'heartbeat' to describe these legislative bans on abortion because it is misleading language, out of step with the anatomical and clinical realities of that stage of pregnancy." and "Pregnancy and foetal development are a continuum; What's interpreted as a heartbeat in these bills is actually electrically induced flickering of a portion of foetal tissue that will become the heart as the embryo develops."

"The flickering that we're seeing on the ultrasound that early in the development of the pregnancy is actually an electrical activity, and the sound that you 'hear' is actually manufactured by the ultrasound machine." - Nisha Verma, an OB-GYN who specializes in abortion care

Controversy exists surrounding six-week abortion bans in part because there is debate on the point at which an embryo's heartbeat can be detected. In 2013, when the Wyoming House of Representatives considered a "heartbeat bill", Norine Kasperik said that "she heard

different answers as] to when a heartbeat is detectable", and in her view "there seemed to be variation by medical equipment used". Mary Throne asked: "Is this abortion illegal at 22 days with a highly invasive ultrasound or is it illegal at 9 weeks when we hear a heartbeat with a stethoscope?" Other critics of the bills have claimed that they ignore that not all embryos' heartbeats become detectable at the same time, even when measured using the same methods. The Centre for Reproductive Rights has stated that there is some inconsistency with regard to these laws; specifically, the Arkansas law requires providers to use an abdominal ultrasound to attempt to detect a foetal heartbeat, while the North Dakota law allows the use of any available technology, including a transvaginal probe, which makes it possible to detect a foetal heartbeat earlier than an abdominal ultrasound scan.
 With specific regard to the North Dakota law, detecting an embryo's heartbeat at six weeks into a pregnancy requires the use of a transvaginal ultrasound, which some members of the abortion-rights movement say is unnecessarily invasive.

CHAPTER 4

Controversy

The leading activist for the passage of six-week abortion ban legislation, and the author of the original

2011 Ohio House Bill 493, was anti-abortion activist Janet Porter. Porter is the founder of the conservative Christian ministry Faith2Action.

Pregnancy from rape

Further information: Pregnancy from rape

It is estimated that there are 25–32 thousand pregnancies from rape per year in adult women, although the number may be considerably higher because many women do not report rape. Most women suffer from post-traumatic stress disorder (PTSD) following the rape and find a decision especially difficult so soon after the trauma of the rape and the physical and mental trauma that they may experience for an extended period of time.

In the United States, there are an estimated 25–32 thousand pregnancies from rape per year in adult women. Many victims receive little to no aftercare and most experience various forms of PTSD. A third of these pregnancies are not discovered until the second trimester. Any delay in detection reduces women's options, especially outside major urban centers, but many women are still recovering from being raped when they are called on to decide whether to have an abortion. It is known that most women do not report sexual assault, and many times it is hard to bring an assault case to trial. Teenage girls are especially unlikely to report an assault, even though 74% of women who had intercourse before age 14 and 60% of those who had sex before age 15 report having had a forced sexual experience. One study conducted in the 1970s that looked at California data found that "on average, only 413 men were arrested annually for statutory rape in California, even though 50,000 pregnancies occurred among underage women in 1976 alone".

Alabama's "heartbeat bill", passed in 2019, makes abortions illegal even in cases of rape and incest. Furthermore, it requires that judges terminate the parental rights of a man convicted of first-degree rape and certain other sex crimes, leaving a loophole that allows rapists to seek custody of a child conceived through their assault. However, because the law requires a conviction, activists say that since most sexual assaults are never reported, much less produce a finding of guilt in court, many victims are left vulnerable. Activists fear that a victim could find herself in a situation where she would be forced to bear a child of rape and then be forced to co-parent the child with her rapist. Responding to criticism of the Texas "heartbeat bill" which also includes women or girls who have been raped, Governor Greg Abbott asserts that the Act will not force a woman who has been raped to carry a pregnancy to term because the state will "work tirelessly to make sure that we eliminate all rapists from the streets of Texas by aggressively going out and arresting them and prosecuting them and getting them off the streets."

Constitutionality

 Constitutionality § Unconstitutional laws in the United States

Critics of six-week abortion bans say that, since Roe v. Wade established that states must allow abortion until the point of viability (between 24 and 28 weeks into the pregnancy), such bills "blatantly contradict" Supreme Court precedent. The 2013 North Dakota law banning abortions after six weeks was ruled by District Court to be "clearly invalid and unconstitutional based on the United States Supreme Court precedent in Roe v. Wade."

Proponents of six-week abortion bans contend that the constitutional precedent of Roe v. Wade should be re-examined in light of advancements in law and science. Ohio Governor Mike DeWine argued that the main purposes of the bills are to "protect the most vulnerable among us, those who don't have a voice" and that the "government's role should be to protect life from the beginning to the end."

CHAPTER 5

"Informed consent" laws

A related though the distinct type of law is that introduced at the state level in all 50 states in the US in October 2011, which would require any woman seeking an abortion to see and hear their conceptus's heartbeat. Supporters included the United States Conference of Catholic Bishops, Americans United for Life, and Susan B. Anthony List. Another such bill was introduced in Texas. A similar type of legislation, the Heartbeat Informed Consent Act, was introduced at the national level around the same time by Michele Bachmann; however, it died in committee. Another law of this variety, introduced by Sharon Weston Broome, was passed by legislators in Louisiana in 2012, as an amendment to a 2010 bill requiring women seeking an abortion to receive an ultrasound of their concepts. Similar laws have been passed in states such as Georgia in 2005; and a law that mandated both an ultrasound of the "unborn child" and listening to its heartbeat before an abortion could be procured was laid on the table in 2012 in Pennsylvania. This last bill became controversial when Tom Corbett, Pennsylvania's governor, stated that "You just have to close your eyes" and dismissed accusations that the bill would be unnecessarily obtrusive. Furthermore, while the anti-abortion movement claims that bills mandating a woman listen to her conceptus' heartbeat would increase the likelihood of them changing their mind, the abortion-rights community, with the support of the Pennsylvania Medical Society, opposes "informed-consent" bills because they threaten to, if passed, "significantly jeopardize the open dialogue within the physician-patient relationship."

"Informed consent" laws requiring women seeking abortions to have the physician play a recording of her conceptus' heartbeat have met with challenges in court, notably in Texas, when the CRR filed a lawsuit against it, leading to a court case entitled Texas Medical Providers Performing Abortion Services v. Lakey.

Prior to Sam Sparks condemning the law in January 2012, however, a federal district court had ruled that the law violated the First Amendment in August 2011. This decision was reversed by the United States Court of Appeals for the Fifth Circuit, led by Edith Jones. Another similar law was challenged in North Carolina in Stuart v. Huff, in which a federal district court ruled that the law was in violation of the First Amendment. This case, unlike the one in Texas, has not yet been appealed. This has led to some debate among different anti-abortion groups regarding strategy; specifically, while some of these groups, like the Kansas Coalition for Life, have supported the passing of this legislation, others, like Kansans for Life, are concerned that "enacting a fetal heartbeat ban would prompt a court ruling undoing some limits on abortion and providers." Paul Linton, a former general counsel for AUL, has argued that foetal heartbeat laws "have no chance in the courts." He, like most mainstream anti-abortion advocates (including James Bopp), prefers instead a legislative strategy that chips away at Roe v. Wade.

CHAPTER 6

Legal challenges

Arkansas lawsuit

On May 27, 2015, the Eighth Circuit Court of Appeals affirmed a lower court ruling and permanently blocked the law from being enforced.

In January 2016, The U.S. The Supreme Court declined to review the case, leaving the Eighth Circuit's ruling in place.

Iowa lawsuit

On May 15, 2018, eleven days after Iowa Governor, Kim Reynolds, signed SF 359 into law, Planned Parenthood of the Heartland, Inc., Jill Meadows, and Emma Goldman Clinic (petitioners) filed a lawsuit seeking declaratory and injunctive relief in state court arguing the foetal heartbeat law violated the Iowa State Constitution.

On June 1, 2018, Polk County District Court Judge Michael Huppert entered a preliminary injunction that temporarily blocked the law from going into effect.

On January 22, 2019, the county district judge declared the law to be in violation of the Iowa Constitution and entered a permanent injunction prohibiting its enforcement. In holding the law unconstitutional the judge cited the Iowa Supreme Court's 2018 ruling in a challenge to a different abortion restriction in which the state's court of last resort held that "a woman's right to decide whether to terminate a pregnancy is a fundamental right under the Iowa Constitution." Anti-abortion proponents have said they hope this litigation creates a pathway for Roe v. Wade to be reexamined by the U.S. Supreme Court, but University of Iowa law professor Paul Gowder and other legal experts have said that it is almost impossible that it could end up in front of the U.S. Supreme Court, as the U.S. The Supreme Court does not review Supreme Court decisions concerning state constitutional questions.

In response to Judge Michael Huppert's ruling that Iowa's heartbeat abortion ban violates the state Constitution, anti-abortion legislators have filed legislation to amend the state constitution to state "that the Constitution of the State of Iowa does not secure or protect a right to or require the funding of abortion."

 The resolutions proposing to amend Iowa's constitution are SJR 9 and HJRwhich were filed on January 24, 2019, and February 6, 2019, respectively.

Kentucky lawsuit

Kentucky already has three lawsuits over abortion restrictions.

North Dakota lawsuit

In July 2015, the Eighth Circuit Court of Appeals affirmed a lower court decision blocking HB 1456 from going into effect.

 The U.S. The Supreme Court declined to review the case and the law remains permanently blocked.

Texas lawsuits

There have been multiple lawsuits challenging the enforcement of the 2021 Texas Heartbeat Act. Several of these are still pending or active.

CHAPTER 7

State Laws

Alabama
On March 4, 2014, the Alabama House passed House Bill 490, which prohibits abortions if a heartbeat is discovered, by a vote of 73-29. As a result, they became the first state to approve such legislation. The measure was eventually killed in committee.
Alabama approved an abortion bill that is more restrictive than a heartbeat law in 2019.
 House Bill 314 was submitted in the House on April 2, 2019, prohibiting abortions at all stages of pregnancy and criminalizing the process for doctors (save in cases of a medical emergency or deadly fetal abnormalities). The measure passed the House on April 30 (74-3), the Senate on May 14,, and Governor Kay Ivey signed it into law on May 16.
Arkansas
A fetal heartbeat measure prohibiting abortion beyond twelve weeks was enacted by the Arkansas Senate on January 31, 2013. It was vetoed in Arkansas by Governor Mike Beebe, but his veto was overcome by the Arkansas House of Representatives on March 6, 2013.
 A federal judge issued a temporary injunction against the Arkansas statute in May 2013,, and it was declared

illegal by federal judge Susan Webber Wright in March 2014.

Florida

In 2019, the Florida Legislature received two foetal heartbeat legislation.

 On January 10, 2019, Rep. Mike Hill introduced a foetal heartbeat bill (HB 235) in the Florida House of Representatives. Sen. Dennis Baxley introduced a companion measure (SB 792) in the Florida Senate on February 6, 2019. The identical bills would have made it a third-degree felony for a doctor to perform an abortion on a woman after a fetal heartbeat is detected, unless the "woman has been diagnosed with a condition that would create a serious risk of significant and irreversible impairment of a major bodily function if the woman delayed terminating her pregnancy." Both measures were killed in committee.

Florida Governor Ron DeSantis has promised to approve legislation prohibiting abortions after the detection of a baby's heartbeat.

Georgia

Georgia House Bill 481 is the main article.

In 2015, two foetal heartbeat laws were introduced in the Georgia General Assembly.

citation required]

On February 25, 2019, Rep. Ed Setzler presented HB 481 in the Georgia House of Representatives.

Sen. Bruce Thompson of Georgia is likely to introduce a similar bill in the Georgia State Senate soon.Brian Kemp, the current Governor of Georgia, declared during his campaign for governor, "vowed to sign the strictest abortion restrictions in the country," and when challenged about legal action, responded, "bring it! I'll fight for my life in the Capitol and court."HB 481 was cleared out of a Senate committee on March 18, 2019, after being passed out of the House on March 7, 2019.It was then approved by the whole state Senate before being narrowly approved by the House 92-78. 0 On May 7, 2019, Governor Kemp signed the measure, putting into force one of the harshest abortion restrictions in the US at the time. 0

The law would make abortion illegal when a heartbeat is found in a conceptus, which is normally when a woman is six weeks pregnant.

Former Georgia governor candidate Stacey Abrams, a Democrat, labelled the law a "forced pregnancy bill." On April 13, 2021, Idaho Rep. Gregory Chaney presented HB 366, which would prohibit abortions when a baby's heartbeat is found. The measure passed the house by a vote of 53-16 on April 16, 2021, and the senate by a vote of 25-7 on April 21, 2021, before being signed into law by Governor Brad Little on April 29, 2021. There were exceptions for rape, incest, and when the mother's life was in danger. The statute takes effect if an appeals court upholds another such prohibitionA better source is required]

Iowa

On May 4, 2018, Governor Kim Reynolds signed legislation prohibiting abortion in Iowa when a baby's heartbeat is discovered, effective July 1, 2018.

On January 22, 2019, a county district court deemed the ordinance unconstitutional and issued a permanent injunction barring its execution.More information on the litigation against Iowa's foetal heartbeat bill may be found in the Iowa Lawsuit section of this page under the topic of the Legal challenges.

Kansas

In February 2013, the bill was introduced and referred to a committee. In March 2013, the measure was introduced in the Kansas House. House Bill 2324 was titled "An Act Prohibiting Abortion of an Unborn Human Individual with a Detectable Fetal Heartbeat." Mark Gietzen, an ardent supporter of such laws, has attempted to gather as many signatures as possible in order to persuade Sam Brownback to call a special session of Congress to review the bill.Gietzen also pushed for a foetal heartbeat statute to be approved during the Kansas legislature's special session on September 3, 2013. In May 2014, HB 2324 died in committee.

Kentucky

In 2019, the Kentucky General Assembly received two measures that aim to outlaw abortions when a fetal heartbeat is discovered.

On January 8, 2019, Sen. Matt Castlen presented SB 9 in the Kentucky Senate.SB 9 was approved by the Kentucky Senate by a vote of 31-6 on February 14, 2019.On February 15, 2019, the measure was introduced in the House.Damon Thayer, the Senate Republican floor leader, said SB 9 was "definitely" a priority for the chamber and that he would be thrilled if it became law and ended up before the United States Supreme Court as a way to overturn Roe v. Wade. "It would be the crowning achievement of my career," he remarked.SB 9 was passed by the Kentucky House on March 14, 2019, by a vote of 71-19.As of April 2019, the ACLU has filed a lawsuit to oppose it, and a federal judge had stopped enforcement pending the district court's final verdict.

Rep. Robert Goforth presented a similar bill in the Kentucky House of Representatives. On January 10, 2019, the Health and Family Services Committee recommended HB 100, which was pre-filed on December 13, 2018.When asked about the heartbeat bill, Rep. Goforth, who announced his candidacy for Governor of Kentucky on the same day the bill was introduced, said he would be pleased if Kentucky or one of the other states considering similar measures enacted such a law and, if challenged in court, took the case to the United States Supreme Court in an attempt to overturn Roe v. Wade. 2

Previous foetal heartbeat measures introduced in Kentucky have failed to gain traction. A foetal heartbeat bill, HB 132, was proposed on January 7, 2014, by Joseph Fischer. On March 19, 2014, the measure was forwarded to the House Health and Welfare Committee, where it died.2 On January 11, 2013, Rep. Fischer submitted the same measure with the same bill number (Hb 132) as in 2012. On February 20, 2013, the measure was forwarded to the House Health and Welfare Committee, where it died. 22

Maryland

In 2019, two foetal heartbeat bills were introduced in the Maryland House of Delegates. Ric Metzgar introduced House Bill 933 on February 8, 2019.On February 8, 2019, Robin L. Grammer, Jr. introduced HB 978, the "Keep Our Hearts Beating Act."
Minnesota
Tim Miller introduced HF 271 in the Minnesota House of Representatives on January 22, 2019.
Mississippi
In Mississippi, three heartbeat legislation was introduced in 2018, all of which failed in committee. In Mississippi, three heartbeat legislation were introduced in 2017, all of which failed in committee.3Sen. Joey Fillingane introduced a heartbeat bill in the Mississippi State Senate in 2014.The measure was killed in committee. 4 HB 6 was presented in January of 2013 and died in committee on February 5, 2013.
On February 5, 2019, HB 529 by Robert Foster, another foetal heartbeat measure introduced in 2019, was lost in the House Judiciary A Committee.
In January 2019, three foetal heartbeat legislation was introduced in the Mississippi Legislature.
 On January 11, 2019, Sen. Angela Burks Hill's SB 2116 was sent to the Public Health and Welfare Committee.
 On January 17, 2019, Rep. Chris Brown's HB was referred to the Public Health and Human Services Committee.
 Both SB 2116 and HB 732 were cleared out of their respective committees on February 5, 2019, and were

passed out of the Mississippi Senate and Mississippi House on February 13, 2019. The Senate agreed to the House modifications to SB 2116 on March 19, 2019,, and Mississippi Governor Phil Bryant signed the foetal heartbeat measure into law on March 22, 2019.
Missouri
On January 9, 2019, two foetal heartbeat legislation was filed in Missouri.
 Sen. Andrew Koenig introduced SB 139 in the Missouri Senate; the bill is currently waiting in the Health and Pensions Committee.
 Rep. Nick Schroer introduced HB 126 in the Missouri House of Representatives.HB 126 was referred to the Children and Families Committee on January 30, 2019, and a public hearing on the measure was held on February 12, 2019.HB 126 was voted out of committee to the full House on February 21, 2018, with the recommendation that it "do approve." HB 126 was passed by the Missouri House and forwarded to the state Senate on February 27, 2019.Missouri House Speaker Elijah Haahr has stated his support for the "heartbeat bill," citing it as a key priority for the 2019 legislative session.5 Governor Mike Parson responded, "I've been pro-life my entire career, and I support it all the time," when asked if he would sign a fetal heartbeat law. 5
The measure was signed on May 24, 2019, and goes into effect on August 28, 2019. Abortions beyond 8 weeks are prohibited under the measure, with no exceptions for rape or incest.

North Dakota HB 1456 was signed into law in March 20136 by North Dakota Governor Jack Dalrymple, who described it as "a reasonable endeavour by a state legislature to determine the limitations of Roe v. Wade." It was swiftly halted by a federal district judge, which concluded that it obviously violated the constitutional rights guaranteed by Roe v. Wade.] In July of that year, the Center for Reproductive Rights (CRR) filed a lawsuit against the statute on behalf of Red River Women's Facility, North Dakota's sole abortion clinic. The measure was halted by the 8th U.S. Circuit Court of Appeals in July 2015. 6 The case was appealed to the Supreme Court, but the court rejected a petition of certiorari in January 2015, upholding the 8th Circuit Court of Appeals' judgement.

Ohio

In Ohio, Janet Porter6 co-authored a foetal heartbeat bill, HB 125, which was submitted to the state assembly in October 2011.

 To avoid controversy, the Republican-majority Senate tabled the bill. Jack Willke was a vocal supporter of this legislation. Janet Porter of Faith2Action wrote the original bill, which former Governor John Kasich vetoed twice before it passed.

In Ohio, John Kasich signed a related law (HB 248) in 2013, which mandates, among other things, that doctors who fail to test for a foetal heartbeat face criminal penalties; specifically, "the doctor's failure to do so would be a first-degree misdemeanour, carrying up to six months in jail, for the first violation and a fourth-degree felony, carrying up to 18 months in jail, for subsequent violations."

 Lynn Wachtmann and others submitted a new foetal heartbeat bill on August 14, 2013, based on Porter's original.

Another heartbeat law (House Bill 69) was passed by the Ohio House of Representatives on March 25, 2015. According to the Guardian, "the bill is unlikely to advance, facing fierce opposition in the Senate as well as from John Kasich, the Republican governor of Ohio."

On December 6, 2016, the Ohio Senate amended an unrelated law, House Bill 493, previously passed by the Ohio House of Representatives, to include a heartbeat ban clause. The bill was restored to the House and passed the next day.Abortion after the detection of a fetal heartbeat would be a fifth-degree crime unless a physician deemed it necessary "to prevent the death of the pregnant woman or to avert a severe danger of the substantial and permanent impairment of a key bodily function of the pregnant woman."On December 13, 2016, Kasich vetoed the law, claiming that it was unconstitutional and would probably likely be overturned in court if challenged.The Ohio House of Representatives debated whether to overturn Kasich's veto, which would need a three-fifths majority in both chambers. However, House leadership chose not to reconvene members in Columbus before the end of the year, assuring Kasich's veto would stand.

The measure was approved by the Ohio Senate with a vote of 21 years and 10 nays out of 33 seats.

In the House of Representatives, the bill passed the Ohio House with a vote of 56 years, out of 99 seats in the house; it received 39 nays

Two foetal heartbeat bills were submitted in the Ohio General Assembly in 2019, marking the fifth time such legislation has been proposed in the state during the 133rd Session of the Ohio General Assembly. 8 Christina Hagan and Ron Hood submitted HB 688 on February 11, 2019, which was presented in the Ohio House of Representatives on February 12, 2019. Kristina Roegner introduced SB 23 in the Ohio Senate on February 12, 2019;the measure was sent to the Health, Human Services, and Medicaid Committee on February 13, 2019.On February 21, 2019, Ohio Senate President Larry Obhof said that SB 23 will be passed out of the upper house by the middle of March, adding, "We are going to pass that measure by the middle of March." "I have absolutely no doubt." SB 23 was approved by the Ohio Senate on March 13, 2019, by a vote of 19 to 13. 8 The measure was changed and approved by the Ohio House the next month, 56-40; the revisions were affirmed by the Senate, 18-13. On April 11, 2019, Governor Mike DeWine signed the measure into law. On July 3, 2019, a federal court temporarily halted the bill's implementation, just days before it was set to take effect.

In April 2012, then-Oklahoma Governor Mary Fallin signed a fetal heartbeat bill (SB 1274), which compels abortion providers to provide a woman the chance to

hear the conceptus' heartbeat before terminating the pregnancy if the conceptus is at least eight weeks old. The measure went into effect in November of 2012.
Pennsylvania
On May 2, 2018, Rep Rick Saccone presented a foetal heartbeat bill (HB 2315) in the Pennsylvania House of Representatives.
The measure was forwarded to the Judiciary Committee for consideration, where it died.
In December 2018, South Carolina State Representative John McCravy introduced HB 3020 in the South Carolina House of Representatives.
The "Fetal Heartbeat Protection from Abortion Act," which was introduced on January 8, 2018, was referred to the House Judiciary Committee. 9 Attempts to enact foetal heartbeat legislation in the South Carolina General Assembly have previously failed. On January 27, 2021, the State Senate voted 30-13 to enact the new prohibition. There were exceptions to the ban in situations of rape, incest, and where the mother's life was in danger.Similar legislation has been enacted by the state's Republican-controlled House in past years.McMaster signed the measure into law on February 18, 2021, but it was overturned a day later by U.S. District Court Judge Mary Geiger Lewis in response to a lawsuit filed by Planned Parenthood and Greenville Women's Clinic.
In 2019, the Tennessee General Assembly received two foetal heartbeat legislation. Rep. James "Micah" Van Huss introduced HB 77 in the Tennessee House of Representatives on January 23, 2019.Sen. Mark Pody

introduced SB 1236 in the Tennessee Senate on February 7, 2019.HB 77 was approved by a Public Health subcommittee and referred to the full committee on February 20, 2019.The House Public Health Committee voted 15-4 on February 26, 2019, to bring HB 77 to the House floor for a full vote.HB 77 was approved by a vote of 66-21 in the Tennessee House on February 7, 2019.

Texas

Texas Heartbeat Act is the main article.

Whole Woman's Health v. Jackson and United States v. Texas are two further cases to consider (2021)

Phil King filed a foetal heartbeat measure in Texas on July 18, 2013, after Rick Perry's signature of Texas Senate Bill 5.

A better source is required] The bill did not pass.1 Representatives Phil King, Dan Flynn, Tan Parker, and Rick Miller co-authored the measure (HB 1500).HB 1500 has 57 sponsors or cosponsors among the 150 members of the Texas House of Representatives as of February 26, 2019.Wendy Davis, a former state senator, called HB 1500 "the most destructive bill I've ever seen."

State senator Bryan Hughes of Mineola, Texas, presented the Texas Heartbeat Measure (SB8) to the Texas Senate on March 11, 2021, while state representative Shelby Slawson of Stephenville, Texas, submitted a similar bill (HB1515) to the state house. There is an exemption for medical crises, but it also covers instances when a mother or girl became pregnant via incest or rape. Governor Greg Abbott claims that the Act would not compel a raped woman to carry a pregnancy to term because the state will "work relentlessly to ensure that we eradicate all rapists from the streets of Texas by aggressively going out and arresting, prosecuting, and getting them off the streets."

The bill's SB8 version was approved by both houses and signed into law by Texas Governor Abbott on May 19, 2021. It will be implemented on September 1, 2021.Instead of the government enforcing the legislation, private persons will be free to sue the provider or anybody who assists the lady in obtaining an abortion. Although similar, H.B NO 1515 should not be confused with bill H.R 705, commonly known as the Heartbeat Protection Act of 2021, presented in Congress on February 2, 2021, and supported by Republican Mike Kelly.Both bills mention the punishment of physicians who conduct abortions after detecting a heartbeat at the 6-week point of a woman's pregnancy. According to the Texas Tribune, "sponsors of the measure believe that this creative clause would stymie legal challenges to the law since without state employees enforcing the prohibition, there will be no one for pro-rights women's organisations to sue."

The expense of being sued is an important factor in the implementation of the HB 1515 statute. According to the introduction legislation, if an organization or person is found guilty of helping in an abortion, each individual faces a minimum $10,000 penalty.In contrast to H.R 705, HB 1515 only discusses punishment via $10,000 penalties, however, if found guilty under H.R 705, doctors are not only susceptible to a fine, but also to jail time.

According to some supporters of HB 1515, the severity of the expense of being sued is deliberate. This link is shown by John Seago, an active legislative director for Texas Right to Life, an anti-abortion group. According to Seago, the risk of being sued might operate as an incentive for abortion physicians to avoid performing abortions. "Have a public statement," Seago told the Texas Tribune. Put it on their website that they're not arranging appointments beyond six weeks,"and those linked with abortion will cease their activity and will no longer be subject to the penalties.

In June 2021, senior class valedictorian Paxton Smith, 18, delivered a high school graduation speech addressing the Texas heartbeat bill rather than the one pre-approved by her school, saying, "I cannot give up this platform to promote complacency and peace, when there is a war on my body and a war on my rights." The speech went viral, with millions of people watching it on YouTube, TikTok, and Twitter.

On October 6, 2021, District Court Judge Robert L. Pitman temporarily stopped the law, but an appeals court panel restored it on October 8.

West Virginia (WV)

In 2019, two foetal heartbeat proposals were presented in the West Virginia House of Delegates. Ralph Rodighiero (D-Logan) introduced HB 2903, titled "The Foetal Heartbeat Act," on February 7, 2019.Evan Worrell (R-Cabell) introduced HB 2915 on February 8, 2019.

Wyoming
Representative Kendell Kroeker sponsored HB 97, a
foetal heartbeat measure, in the Wyoming House of
Representatives in January 2013. In February 2013, a
house committee voted 4-5 to kill the measure.

MY VIEW CONCERNING THE NEW LAW

Going straight to the point,i really think the law is a
bad idea